I Am Ezer

The Glory of a Woman

Michelle Harrell

ISBN 979-8-88832-377-9 (paperback)
ISBN 979-8-88832-378-6 (digital)

Christian Faith Publishing
832 Park Avenue
Meadville, PA 16335
www.christianfaithpublishing.com

Printed in the United States of America

Endorsements

Where do I start with Michelle? She is the queen of my heart. She *is* my heart. My journey with her has been wonderful and joyous. I would not be anything without her. This book tells some of our story, some of His story with the two of us as the main characters. Lola, as I call her many times, has been the well of wisdom from which I draw often. When I was introduced to her, I was hurting and empty. I knew Jesus, but I did not *know* Jesus—head knowledge, not heart knowledge. At a certain point in our relationship, I faced this truth and the swirling void of my sin. Michelle and my sweet future in-laws knelt with me in prayer as I cried out to the Savior for salvation and deliverance. Salvation was immediate. Deliverance was to come later. My prayer is that this book will be a springboard for new ground in the lives of all who read it. This book is not just for the ladies. Men will find they are not alone in the struggle with pornography and the self-loathing that washes into the wake of this horrible habit. Men will benefit from seeing a woman's point of view on this issue. Humble yourself as I have had to do many times, and let the Holy Spirit instruct you in the pages of this book. You will be delivered into peace and rest.

—Brian Harrell (Michelle's man)

I am so glad you hold this book in your hand by the author Michelle Harrell. She has written a blatantly honest book about her and Brian's struggles in their marriage. Take these precepts and suggestions shared by Michelle, and put them to work in your life today.

We all have a past, whether it was caused by something we did, something someone else did to us, or a combination of both. There comes a time when our past must face resolution. In this book, *I Am Ezer: The Glory of a Woman*, Michelle lays out powerful steps based on biblical principles to help each of us move toward a life pleasing to Jesus—the healer of all our hurts. Are you ready to embark on such an honest and committed journey? If so, then you have a straightforward resource to guide you.

We are Randy and Connie Cheek. We have been married for over fifty years. We love Michelle and Brian. I am the senior pastor of the church they attend. What Michelle writes is not easy to do but worth the effort. Our prayer for you is that God will transform your life and your marriage.

—Randy M. Cheek, DMin
Senior Pastor, Eastwood Baptist Church,
Marietta, Georgia

Raw. Vulnerable. Hopeful. Inspiring.

If you're looking for a fairy-tale marriage book, this is not the one for you. But let's be honest; many of the secular, untrue, and unrealistic pictures of marriage have paved the way for the disappointment and dissatisfaction that many feel in their marriages today.

In this book, she candidly shares the struggles that she and Brian have faced—struggles all too familiar to many people. But she doesn't stop with her honesty; she then shares a path forward. It's a path of prayer, of possibility, and of a glorious marriage.

I've known Michelle my entire life. My wife, Laura, and I have watched her and Brian practice what they preach. In our first few years of marriage, I'm thankful to have the model of people like Brian and Michelle! If you will follow the biblical model that Michelle shares, you'll be on your way to a more meaningful marriage and a closer walk with God.

—Kevin Scott
Executive Pastor, Eastwood Baptist Church
Entrepreneur and Author of *The Lepers Lessons*, *The Lens of Leadership*, and *8 Essential Exchanges*

Michelle has had an anointing on her life since the day she was born. Her desire for studying God's Word and teaching it is amazing to me. In this book, she has taught me much more than I have ever or will ever teach her as her mother. If you are interested in being the helpmeet and lady warrior that God wants you to be, then I know this book will help you achieve your goal.

—Clara Tidwell (Michelle's mom)

Ezer Kenegdo? Once, it was just a Hebrew word I have never heard before. Today, it is a daily pursuit esteemed with great honor. My favorite storyteller of all time has captured her passion and expressed it beautifully within these pages.

—Mandy Christie (lifelong best friend)
Board Member, Glorious Marriage Revolution
Team Member, Inner Court Sanctuary

This book made me laugh and cry. Regardless of your stage in life, it will inspire and challenge you. Michelle gives a candid look into her own life, the lessons she has learned, and how God has delivered her from the enemy's lies time after time. The "Questions for Thought" and the "Call to Action" throughout the book inspired me to examine my own life and relationship with God. She is a Jesus warrior and a captivating teacher, giving Bible stories life as she teaches us what God says about *us*—specifically you…specifically me. I recommend reading with a highlighter in hand.

—Tara Bomar (lifelong best friend)

Michelle and I have walked through many stages of life together over the past twenty-seven years. More times than I can count, usually over a cup of coffee on her couch, she has helped me look to God's Word for some pretty big life issues. As I read this book, I am encouraged once again by my precious friend that I am the mighty warrior God designed me to be and that I can walk in that identity. If you need renewed hope for any part of your life, settle into your comfy place with a cup of coffee and expect to hear from God through this book!

—Donna Parker (lifelong best friend)

If you want to know your true God-given purpose in your marriage, this is the book for you. Michelle shares how to become a true ezer warrior for your husband. She teaches how to pray and claim God's promises to protect our families from the enemy. A quick read but mighty in truth.

—Leigh Ann Whiting (lifelong best friend)
Team Member, Inner Court Sanctuary Prayer

Michelle Harrell is the real deal. As her best friend for forty-plus years, I can testify that her love for Jesus is genuine and contagious. She is real and raw, and you will see her truth and her heart in the pages of this book. Michelle is truly an ezer to Brian every day, and I am thankful to her for being a vessel that the Lord has used and will continue to use to help so many women as she has helped me. I recommend this book to every woman breathing to learn who she was created to be and to help her become an equipped and empowered warrior—an ezer.

—Melissa Womack Adams (lifelong best friend)

Michelle is a teacher, leader, and writer who extracts the truth of God's Word through the guidance of the Holy Spirit. This remarkable and powerful book is proof that she sees the needs of others and profoundly touches their lives through God's promises.

—Pilar Garner
Board Member, Glorious Marriage Revolution
Prayer Team Leader, Inner Court Sanctuary

What a gift this book is! Michelle's words have been soaked in countless hours of study in God's Word and are full of grace and mercy. This book will have you highlighting something on just about every page and reading parts of it out loud to yourself. It's just that profound!

—Penny Bentley
Board Member, Glorious Marriage Revolution
Prayer Team Member, Inner Court Sanctuary

Friend, you will never look at yourself or your marriage the same again after reading this book. Wow! Even if you are a single lady, you need to read this Holy Spirit–inspired book. It will reveal to you, through God's Word, just how powerful you are in Christ, and you will gain a greater understanding of your unique place in the kingdom. A *must*-read for *all* women!

—Ann Rakestraw
Board Member, Glorious Marriage Revolution
Prayer Team Member, Inner Court Sanctuary

I Am Ezer: The Glory of a Woman is a must-read for every woman in every season of life. The covenant of marriage between one man and one woman is under attack. The enemy is on the loose running to and fro looking for individuals and marriages to devour. This book is a timely word equipping women to truly understand who and by whom they were created to be—their spiritual DNA. Michelle's transparency and vulnerability in her marriage testimony are sure to help set women free—married, single, divorced, and widowed alike. Her passion for the Gospel comes alive on the pages much like it does when she's on a platform teaching. *I Am Ezer* does not disappoint. By the final word, women everywhere will band together, confidently suit up in their new equipping, and send up a war cry. Devil, you can't have our women—wives, mothers, sisters, and daughters—for WE ARE EZER!

—Lisa Thompson
Board Member, Glorious Marriage Revolution
Prayer Team Member, Inner Court Sanctuary

Michelle is a blessing to the body of Christ. God has anointed her for this reason and, for this season, to teach women how to fight the real enemy. From her in-depth study of God's Word and life experiences, she is equipped by Holy Spirit to teach you, my fellow ezers. So go ahead and take the journey through this book. You will be blessed and empowered. The breath of God is on this book!

—Linda O'Cain
Board Member, Glorious Marriage Revolution
Prayer Team Member, Inner Court Sanctuary

A love story that portrays a glorious marriage, inspired by the Author and Finisher of our Faith. Michelle has been chosen to illustrate this book, not by pictures but by words. The book comes to life as she literally teaches us through the written word. Michelle has been set apart, sustained by His power and grace. Her desire for everyone reading this is for them to return to their First Love and use this book to write their love story and ultimately have a glorious marriage.

—Amy Brown
Board Member, Glorious Marriage Revolution
Prayer Team Member, Inner Court Sanctuary

How to Have a
Personal Relationship with Jesus

Before we even get started in this book I want to ask you, my sweet friend, do you have a personal relationship with Jesus? If you do not, please don't turn the page until you read this!

Many believe that being raised in church or going to church makes them a Christian. It doesn't make you a Christian, it makes you part of a religion. Many even think that baptism alone, even as a child or as an adult, makes them a Christian. It does not. It just made you wet. Jesus didn't come to make you part of a religion; He came to have a personal relationship with you.

John 3:16 tells us that, "God so loved the world that He gave His one and only Son, that whoever believes in Him shall not perish but have eternal life."

Romans 5:8 says, "God demonstrated His own love for us in this: while we were still sinners, Christ died for us."

Jesus, the Son of God, came as a man to sacrifice His own life for us because none of us are good enough to ever stand before a Holy God. Romans 3:10 tells us, "There is no one righteous, no not one." Isaiah 64:6 tells us that our righteousness is as filthy rags. None of us are good enough to ever make it into heaven on our own apart from the blood of Jesus. Ephesians 2:8–9 says this: "For it is by grace you have been saved, through faith—and this is not from yourselves, it is the gift of God—not by works, so that no one can boast."

> But when the kindness and love of God our Savior appeared, He saved us, not because of righteous things we had done, but because of His mercy. He saved us through the washing of rebirth and renewal by the Holy Spirit, whom He poured out on us generously through Jesus Christ our Savior, so that, having been justified by His grace, we might become heirs having the hope of eternal life. (Titus 3:4–7)

You might want to read that again, slowly.

The good news of Jesus Christ is so simple, even a little child can understand it. We are sinners. We are not good enough to get to God or go to heaven on our own. We need a savior, and that savior is Jesus. Romans 10:9–10 lays it out so perfectly: "If you confess with your mouth, 'Jesus is Lord', and believe in your heart that God raised Him from the dead, you will be saved. For it is with your heart that you believe and are justified, and it is with your mouth that you confess and are saved." Our God is so merciful and so kind. He tells us in 1 John 1:9, "If we confess our sins, he is faithful and just and will forgive us our sins and purify us from all unrighteousness."

It is as simple as telling God that you know you're a sinner. Tell Him you believe that Jesus is the Son of God, that He is Lord and that He died on the cross for your sin, and that He was raised from the dead. Confess with your mouth and believe in your heart, and you will be saved. He will come into your heart! He will forever live within you and, one day, will take you home to heaven and proclaim before the Father, "This is one of Mine!"

If you prayed to receive Jesus as your Savior, the heavens are rejoicing over you right now!

> I tell you, there is rejoicing in the presence of the angels of God over one sinner who repents. (Luke 15:10)

I rejoice with you. Now go tell someone. Tell your pastor or a believing friend. Tell everyone. Get involved in a Bible-teaching church so that you can start growing in your relationship with Jesus. He wants you to have an intimate relationship with Him now. There is nothing sweeter than getting to know Jesus more and more each passing day.

For Those Who Struggle with Doubting Their Salvation and Need Assurance

It is a common thing for us to doubt our salvation. We worry we were not sincere enough or that we didn't pray just the right way. My friend, if you have confessed with your mouth and believe in your heart that Jesus is Lord and that God raised Him from the dead, then the Word says you are saved! God is so kind, and He knew we would have moments of doubt, so He put these verses in His Word so we can know that we *know* we are saved and not ever have to doubt. Read these slowly, and drink deeply of their truth.

Jesus Himself said this in John 10:28, "I give them eternal life, and they shall never perish; no one can snatch them out of my hand. My Father, who has given them to me, is greater than all; no one can snatch them out of my Father's hand. I and the Father are one."

> And this is the testimony: God has given us eternal life, and this life is in His Son. He who has the Son has life; He who does not have the Son of God does not have life. I write these things to you who believe in the name of the Son of

God so that you may know that you have eternal life. (1 John 5:11–13)

Therefore, there is now no condemnation to those who are in Christ Jesus. (Romans 8:1)

Now rest, my friend, and know.

Suggestions for Using
This Book in a Group Study

I desire that as you read this book, you will be drawn to the book of all books—the Bible. It is the perfect Word of God. Neither this book nor any other book will be able to help you like the Bible. If this book or any other book doesn't point you back to the Word of God, put it down. With that said, I have done my best to follow the Holy Spirit as He guided me to specific scriptures to write this book.

This book, of course, can be read on your own, but it is designed so that you can do it with a group of friends if you choose to. I have added sections at the end of each chapter called "Questions for Thought" and "Call to Action." If you read this book with a group of friends, I encourage you to be willing to be open and vulnerable as you answer the questions together. Listen respectfully and without judgment to those in your group. Be trustworthy so that everyone feels they can share without it being repeated to anyone outside the group. I have found that, as women, we learn from each other when we are willing to be open and tell what God has brought us through and where He has brought us from. Too many times we are ashamed of our past, and we don't want to tell anyone. Sharing God's faithfulness and being willing to share even the ugly parts of our lives will build the faith of our other sisters in Christ. My prayer, as the author, is that as I share some of my "ugly" at the beginning of this book you will be encouraged to share yours. Sharing our ugly doesn't mean wallowing in the past; it is rejoicing in God's faithfulness to redeem us and set us free.

Introduction

Hello, friend. My name is Michelle Harrell, and my glorious man is Brian. We have a ministry called Glorious Marriage Revolution, otherwise known as GMR. The idea that marriage can be glorious was birthed by my husband and I through our marriage journey before we ever knew there would be an audience to share it with. I will share more of our story later. First, let me share how this ministry started.

In December 2017, I attended a leadership conference in Las Vegas, Nevada called Oolapalooza. During the time we were there, we discussed seven specific areas of life that we all get out of balance. We looked at where we'd been in those areas and set goals for where we want to be. As we worked through the process that weekend, I had no idea what the Lord was about to do in my life. I went to this leadership conference thinking I was there for a completely different reason. I was working with a company at the time that I felt the Lord wanted me to pursue, and I was answering all the questions with the idea in mind that I would set goals surrounding the growth of my business. One of the speakers mentioned that many of us had dreams or desires that we had as children, and for some reason or another, life had squelched those dreams and we pushed them down within us. He encouraged us to remember those dreams, and he asked us to write them down.

I had a sickening feeling in my gut and had no desire to write down what popped into my mind. This same speaker repeated this to us several more times, and each time, I refused to write down what had been my dream. I have a wonderful life and have seen many of my dreams and heart's desires come to pass. How could I write down this one ridiculous dream that seemed so unattainable and silly to me? During the last weekend's session, he mentioned it one last time and gave us one last opportunity to write down that dream. With my heart pounding and my hands sweating, I wrote down, "I am supposed to be a public speaker," then fought the urge to go to the bathroom and throw up.

Understand that I have no problem with standing in front of an audience and speaking. The bigger the crowd, the more I love it. My urge to throw up came from not having a platform. I mean, you have to have a platform to be a public speaker. I didn't have a platform (or so I thought)! I loved teaching the Word of God and taught a large Sunday school at my church, but I truly thought that's all I would ever do. You can't just go to someone and say, "I love to teach the Bible. Let me teach for you!" I asked the Lord, "What am I supposed to do with this?" Then we left Las Vegas and got back to life.

Ten days after getting home, I had to go pick up my eldest son from his job at Chick-fil-A. While I waited for him, the thought came to mind to get on Facebook live and see who might want to do a book study with me on *The Power of a Praying Wife* by Stormie Omartian. This book changed my life in the nineties and ultimately changed my marriage and how I prayed for my man.

In 2017, I had done several Facebook live videos on my page about some of the things I had learned from this book, and my heart wanted to share with other women how God used this book to change how I prayed for my husband. I jumped on Facebook live without hesitation, thinking that maybe twenty-five to thirty people might join me. I never dreamed it would turn into a revolution! Immediately, people started responding and saying they wanted to join in. That evening, my niece, Hannah, and I created a private Facebook page for the book study and set a start date for January 8, 2018, to give everyone time to get their books.

Within twenty-four hours, there were over 50 women. I was shocked and super excited. Within a week, there were 287 women. In another week, we jumped to 550 women. Reports were coming in that local stores were selling out of the book. Amazon even sold out at one point. I started realizing the hunger in women to simply have a good marriage. They needed hope that it was even possible.

At that point our number was over three thousand strong. My head was spinning. My mind immediately went back to a phone call from my husband several months before. He told me to look up Amos 9:13 in the Message.

Yes indeed, it won't be long now.

God's decree:

> Things are going to happen so fast
> your head will swim, one thing fast on
> the heels of the other. You won't be able
> to keep up. Everything will be happening
> at once—and everywhere you look bless-
> ings! Blessings like wine pouring off the
> mountains and hills.

God was truly on the move. Only *He* could do something like this—by our start date of January 8, 2018, we had 7,771 women. Only God.

And the revolution began.

Acknowledgments

In most books, acknowledgments come before the introduction; however, my acknowledgments wouldn't make sense if my introduction hadn't come first. Before I give one word of acknowledgment to anyone, I must give all glory and honor to my Jesus. His sweet Holy Spirit has ordered every single step even when I had no idea of the magnitude of what this would become. In the first week, I asked participants to answer three questions so I would know better how to pray for them as we got started.

1. How many years have you been married?
2. What condition is your marriage in, currently?
3. Do you have a personal relationship with Jesus Christ?

As the messages started to roll in with answers to these questions and as the numbers swelled almost by the hour, it quickly became apparent that I could not do this alone. I was beautifully overwhelmed by the response to the questions and the hurt that so many women were experiencing. I would read each message and weep. I couldn't take it all in. God knew my heart and my desire to love and serve each of these women that came into the group, but I wasn't able to answer everyone the way I wanted to, so He began to build a team around me to help.

My niece, Hannah Stephens, was my first helper. She was the creator of our Facebook page, and she helped me articulate the vision that God was giving me. My lifelong friend, Melissa Adams, stepped in to help me with administrative demands and eventually helped me respond to all the many messages that flooded in. Melissa and Hannah both helped with responding to messages while I tried to see the ones I felt the Holy Spirit wanted me to respond personally. Soon, the Lord added my sweet friend Jenny Williams to our team. She was invaluable in helping us get many details taken care of as we quickly had to learn how to manage a ministry that was exploding.

It wasn't long until we all realized we needed a prayer team! Prayer requests poured in daily, and we needed a team to help us storm the throne room on behalf of these women. God gave us a strong core of prayer warriors, headed up by Pilar Garner. They are now known as the GMR Inner Court Sanctuary. They are a force to be reckoned with.

Just as I never dreamed that a book study would turn into a full-blown ministry, in my wildest imagination, I never thought I would write a book. If you've ever heard me teach or speak, you know I'm just me, and I say what comes into my brain. It was comical to me to even think of writing a book. Who on earth would want to read a book by me? I am a country girl and as *podunk* as they come! Oh, but God knows us, and His great plans for us are far better than we can fathom. I want to praise Him right here for His endless patience with me while I struggled to believe that I could do this and many days just wanted to throw in the towel. His mercies are new every morning, and great is His faithfulness.

I am forever grateful to my sweet man, Brian, who encouraged me and believed that I could do this, even on my lowest days. He always has my back and is always in my corner.

I am thankful to my parents, Charles and Clara Tidwell. They have been telling me for years that I should write a book. Words have power, that's for sure. They have always believed in me and encouraged me. They were, and still remain, my greatest prayer team ever. They are truly the patriarchs of GMR. They lived a glorious marriage before me and my brothers our entire lives.

I am thankful for my prayer team: Pilar Garner, Penny Bentley, Lisa Thompson, Mandy Christie, Amy Brown, Ann Rakestraw, Linda O'Cain, and Leigh Ann Whiting. They have prayed for me and have allowed me to bounce ideas and thoughts at them throughout this entire process. It surely takes a village.

Chapter 1

Our Story

After two years of dating, Brian and I married on December 8, 1990. I was nineteen, and he was about to turn twenty-one. We were young and in love. He was in the marine reserves and had just been hired as a full-time firefighter. I can truly say his love for me is what caused me to fall in love with him. Sort of like how Jesus first loved us and drew us to Himself, then we realize we love Him. Yes, very much like that.

Just like any young, newly married couple, we had to learn how to be married, how to give and take, and what true intimacy was. But the enemy already had a hold on us, and we didn't even realize it.

Brian had been exposed to pornography as a young kid. It's the story of many men in our society today. Being in the marines didn't help. There were no cell phones or computers back then, but there were plenty of magazines and VHS tapes, and those got passed around. Brian ended up with some of them. He suggested we watch some of the tapes together thinking it would spice things up. Let me insert here that this is not the way to spice things up. It is a recipe for disaster. But I was young and only knew that I wanted to keep my husband happy. He was young and had no idea of the destruction this was eventually going to cause. So we watched a few from time to time. I never felt right about it, and we eventually stopped watching them together, but Brian kept watching. The magazines continued to be passed around. The enemy wasn't just lurking nearby; he was all the way in.

One day, I had some reason to look for something in Brian's bags that he took to the fire station. At the bottom of the bag, under all his clothes, I found the magazines and a few tapes. A hot flush ran through my body, and my heart pounded out of my chest. I felt as if I had just walked in and found him in bed with another woman. I was broken and devastated. I have never been one to hold back my feelings, so I went straight to him to question him about what I had found. He didn't try to backpedal his way out of it, and he faced my hurt and fury head-on. Believe me I was like a hurricane with full-force winds. I screamed, I cried, and I called him names. I did everything I could, verbally, to shame him so that he could feel just a small portion of the shame and betrayal that I was feeling. Needless to say, I wasn't extending mercy and forgiveness. I was hurt, and all I saw was red, and it wasn't the red blood of Jesus.

One thing Brian and I have always had in our favor is good communication. As we continued to talk (well, I screamed mostly), I asked him if it had ever occurred to him that those girls he saw were someone's daughter, someone's sister, possibly even someone's mother! He stared at me with a look of sudden realization. He said he had truly never even thought of that. It wasn't until the Lord started GMR that I realized the way the enemy keeps men bound in the dark with his lies. I also realized that he keeps women bound by their hurt.

As time passed, I made sure to hold this over Brian's head. As much as I loved him, I wanted to somehow make him hurt the way I did. So I used my words and attitude to cut him as deeply as I could. By God's mighty grace, He set Brian free from pornography, but the enemy is always lurking about, waiting to pounce after a victory. And this time, I was his target. As soon as the chains dropped off Brian, the enemy snatched them and put them on me. I was bound so tightly by my unforgiveness and my hurt. I could not get past the shame and betrayal I felt. I told no one. I was raised in church from nine months before I was born. I knew no one who had ever dealt with anything like this. Sadly, no one in church ever talked about their past and what they had been through, so the fear of someone judging me or thinking badly of Brian was overpowering.

Time moved on, and I got deeply involved in leading and facilitating a ladies' Bible study at my church. I also started teaching a ladies' Sunday school. I was growing in my walk with Jesus, but I was still bound in my chains.

Brian always worked two jobs and wasn't able to come to church much. As I grew toward Jesus, he went the other way. He was saved, and he loved Jesus, but he wasn't walking with him. Depression started creeping over him. He became a different person, and I couldn't understand what was wrong. Sometime during all this, *The Power of a Praying Wife* came into my hands. I can't even remember how I came across it. I do, however, remember thinking that I was going to learn how to pray for Brian and get him "fixed." My spiritual system was shocked when I read the first chapter, "His Wife." It talked about allowing the Lord to work on me first. I argued with the Lord and told Him I wasn't the one that needed fixing, then I came to the part that said, "Shut up and Pray." The wind went right out of my sails. I was undone before the Lord. That is when everything changed for me and how I prayed for Brian. My prayer life would never be the same.

This book became part of everything I did. It stayed with my Bible and went with me everywhere I went. I read through the book, then went back and asked the Lord each day what area in his life Brian needed prayer for. Every time I felt the Lord leading me to pray from the chapter "His Temptations," I cringed, and the enemy laughed and pulled my chains tighter. As I prayed, I had to fight all the feelings and memories that came up. The Lord began to teach me that prayer wasn't just about getting what you want or begging Him to fix something for you. It's a battle; it's hard. And it's where the enemy fights us the hardest. If we choose our weapons wisely, it's our greatest place of victory. The Lord started giving me victory in small ways while I learned, ever so slowly, to trust Him as I prayed.

It was a long journey that the Lord took me on, and to be perfectly transparent (you'll find that I am very transparent!), He still has me on it. However, I have learned a few things along the way. I learned that Brian isn't my enemy, and I learned that I am not the Holy Spirit. We all have a very real enemy, and we must learn to fight in prayer and through the Word of God to remind him that he's already a defeated foe. This one thing I know, you *can* have a glorious marriage. It *is* possible. So let's link arms, dive in together, and learn how to fight the real enemy.

Questions for Thought

1. What is your story? Have you been hurt in your marriage? Or have you been the one to cause hurt?
2. Did this hurt cause divorce, or are you on the brink of divorce?
3. If you're single, whether never married, divorced, or widowed, have you experienced hurt so deep that instead of forgiving, you just wanted to retaliate?

4. Do you feel you've never really learned how to pray? Do you know what it means to "fight the real enemy?"

Call to Action

Pray and pour out your heart to the Lord. If you don't know how to fight the real enemy, tell Him. Ask Him to teach you how and then be open and willing to listen for His voice through His Word. God isn't looking for perfect words in prayer. He's looking for a genuine heart.

Chapter 2

Don't Be like Jonah!

Or do you show contempt for the riches of His kindness, tolerance, and patience, not realizing that God's kindness leads you to repentance?

—Romans 2:4

Reading *The Power of a Praying Wife* launched me into a new way of prayer altogether, not just for Brian. It taught me how to pray the Word of God in every area of my life. I was never taught to pray scripture, so as I learned slowly to do this, it also made the Bible come alive for me. It made me want to dive in more and more to see what else I could learn. In time, I realized that the Holy Spirit was my very own personal teacher and that I didn't have to rely on others to teach me the Word. I realized I could learn it straight from the Holy Spirit Himself. That was thrilling to me!

As I continued to pray and learn from the Lord, I began to see changes in Brian, very specific changes that I had prayed for; and by specific, I mean right down to the very words I had prayed. Slowly, the Lord began to transform me and Brian. Looking back, my transformation took much longer. I learned in becoming a prayer warrior that prayer draws you closer to the Savior, and the closer you get, the more it's like looking at yourself in a magnified makeup mirror. You look at yourself and think, *Whoa, is that really what I look like?*

I started to see the ugly parts of myself that I never even knew were there, and I didn't like it. I would often walk away from the mirror and try to ignore that I had just seen that particular thing about myself. If I didn't talk about it, who would ever know? So ignoring it seemed best. But the Lord says in Zechariah 13:9 that He will "refine them as silver is refined, and try them as gold is tried; they shall call on My name and I will hear them: I will say, 'It is my people: and they shall say, 'The Lord is my God.'" He was refining me, bringing the dross to the top until He could see His reflection, all the while hearing me every time I called out to Him and drawing me closer and closer.

As our great God brought Brian out of the dark place he was in and put a new song in his heart, I could visibly see the changes. I was thrilled but continued to resist what the Lord was doing in me. I was continuously crippled by my fear that he would fall back into pornography. I watched his every move, and I made it miserable for both of us when the enemy brought it to mind, which was often. As I prayed for Brian and saw great changes in him, the Lord used those changes to help Brian lead me out of my bondage.

I smile as I write this because I marvel at how gracious the Lord is and how He works. This is such a beautiful picture of a glorious marriage, and He meant it to be. Both the husband and the wife die to themselves to help the other one live. In the times I was most overcome by the lies of the enemy and I allowed those lies to cloud my reasoning, Brian would patiently allow me to pierce him with my accusations and past hurts. He never lashed back at me and never got angry with me. He was only always patient. He started taking his Bible to work with him again and began listening to sermons, as many as he could. I'm praying and seeing all these changes in him, and yet I had set up camp in my anger, fear, and hurt and refused to budge.

I think I might have looked somewhat like Jonah to the Lord. Jonah was told to preach repentance to the city of Nineveh and ran from the Lord. That put him in the belly of a stinky fish for three days. When he finally surrendered to go and the city repented, Jonah was mad! It's comical to read really, but that is what I was doing. I had asked the Lord to make major changes in Brian, and He did, but I was sulking over the things I thought he shouldn't be let off the hook so easily for. Somehow I still wanted him to hurt as I did. My transformation began with the Christlike sweetness of my man.

Romans 2:4 says that the kindness of God leads to repentance. That is exactly what my man showed me. He loved me even when I was so angry, so judgmental, and so fearful just like Jesus died for us while we were yet in our sins. Brian showed patience with me. He would gently tell me, "Michelle, you are listening to lies." The first time he said that to me, it was as if hot water was being poured over ice. Parts of the fear and anger started to melt. I started to feel the chains loosen, and over time, I was free! And it all started with me thinking I needed to pray for Brian and "fix" him. The Lord must've chuckled and thought, "Oh, We have some work to do on you first, child!"

Questions for Thought

1. Have you been praying for your husband or someone else but you're choosing to camp out in your anger and fear?

2. Are you behaving as Jonah did and sulking as you see God doing great things around you, and yet you won't step out of your own pain long enough for Him to set you free?
3. Are you willing to die to yourself, even though you've been hurt?

Call to Action

Ask the Lord to help you step out of your hurt and anger and melt your hard heart. Ask Him to show you how He is working all around you in answer to prayers you've prayed. Stop listening to the lies of the enemy and let the Healer set you free.

Chapter 3

Your Husband Ain't Your Enemy!

For our struggle is not against flesh and blood, but
against the rulers, against the authorities, against
the powers of this dark world and against the
spiritual forces of evil in the heavenly realms.

—Ephesians 6:12

One Sunday after church, I was on the phone with Brian while he was at the fire station. I was excitedly telling him about a new sermon series they were going to do at church on spiritual warfare. Brian had just started reading his Bible again and was getting back into church and watching sermons whenever he could, but this conversation on spiritual warfare disturbed him. He believed it was hokey. We continued to talk, and after a while, he said, "I guess I realize spiritual warfare is real, but I've just never been taught how to fight!" That statement turned a light on in my spirit.

See, the devil doesn't care if you believe he exists or not. He would just as soon you believe that he's a made-up character that is portrayed in movies. Whether you think him to be a funny little character in a red suit, horns, and a pitchfork or you think him to be the evil in the horror movies, he doesn't care. He surely doesn't want you to believe that spiritual warfare is real. Keeping you blinded and distracted from all this is what he feeds on. He doesn't want you to know truth.

The Bible says in John 8:44 that our enemy is a liar and the father of lies and that lying is his native language. John 10:10 says he comes only to steal, kill, and destroy and one of his favorite places to do this is in marriage. That same verse also says Jesus comes so that we may have life and have it more abundantly, and a glorious marriage is part of that abundant life. Sadly, the enemy has lied to so many couples, and he has them believing that an abundant life isn't possible, much less a glorious marriage. The enemy has a scheme, according to Ephesians 6:11. One of his greatest schemes is to keep people living in defeat, to keep husbands and wives at odds with each other all the time, and to steal the God-ordained territory of marriage.

The enemy started his thieving way back in the beginning when marriage first started, but we will get to that in a minute. Let's just look at our current day for now. Most little girls have dreams of a man sweeping her off her feet, a knight in shining armor that will make her heart skip and take her breath away. It'll be just like the movies, right? One day, if all goes somewhat according to plan, she meets "the one," they fall in love, get engaged, post all the appropriate social media engagement photos, and then the wedding plans begin. Everything must be perfect. The world makes much ado about the wedding but doesn't prepare the young couple for the battlefield that is ahead.

No one tells them that the enemy is crouching at the door to burst their picture-perfect bubble. No one tells them that after they take off their wedding attire, they must then adorn themselves with their armor. No one tells them that it's time to go into the trenches after the wedding because they have an enemy to fight. This enemy wants to make them think that they are each other's enemies. No one teaches them how to fight the real enemy together and not fight each other.

We can all well remember our newlywed days. In the first several months, there is much joy and loads of passion, and the newness of life together overshadows any arguments or spats that come up. But as time goes on and the responsibilities of life settle in, the movie-like fairy tale becomes reality. Maybe the lovely bride gets comfortable and starts to gain a little weight, and she might wear those worn-out T-shirts and sweatpants a little too often. Maybe she doesn't fix up as often as she did before the wedding, and now the handsome groom starts to get a little dull in his feelings for her. Or maybe, he doesn't put the seat down after he goes to the bathroom and leaves her a "shower gift" on the toilet and floor. Maybe he doesn't clean up his whiskers in the sink after shaving or clean up the toothpaste spit after brushing his teeth. At first, all this is kind of endearing because the "new" is still there and the bride can sigh, smile, clean it up, and move on. But as it continues, and she has to pick up socks and underwear all the time, maybe it becomes less and less endearing and more and more irritating. The edge gets sharper and sharper. Bills are coming in, jobs get exhausting, and babies won't stop crying. Communication gets muddled, spats turn into fights, and soon they are like roommates. And the enemy laughs knowing he has them right where he wants them.

Marriage is a prime target for our enemy. Newly married or seasoned marriages are all the same to him. He just wants to break them up. Why does he want to break them up? Because marriage is the first institution God ever created. The covenant of marriage and the institution of the family both reflect the glorious relationship we have with the Lord. When it is done according to God's direction, we reflect His glory to an unbelieving world. Without ever saying a word, our marriages can show Jesus to the lost and broken. However, no one comes into marriage or a relationship with Jesus automatically knowing how to fight spiritual warfare. And so, like any good warrior, we need to know our enemy and train ourselves on how to best defeat him. Let's get to it.

Questions for Thought

1. Do you believe Satan exists?
2. Have you heard of spiritual warfare, or is this a new concept to you?
3. Does Brian's struggle sound familiar to you? Maybe you know it's real, but you've just never known how to fight.

Call to Action

Pray and ask the Lord to give you the Spirit of wisdom and understanding, and to open the eyes of your heart so that you may know Him better (Ephesians 1:17–18). Ask Him to help you daily to put on the full armor of God so that you can know how to fight and stand against the schemes of the devil (Ephesians 6:11).

Chapter 4

Ezer Kenegdo: Your Spiritual DNA

Warning: This chapter may feel like you're reading from a college theological textbook, but hang in there with me.

Since the Genesis story, from the time the serpent deceived Eve in the garden, the lies started, and the attempt to demolish a woman's true spiritual DNA began. Truth dispels lies. The word *dispel* means "to make a doubt, feeling or belief disappear." Let's dispel some lies and reveal the truth of what God intended for women to be. It is not what the world or the church has made us out to be.

The world has so twisted the role of women in society that we have a rampant "feminist" movement that bashes men and tries to make women superior. Men and women were *both* created to be image bearers of the Triune, Most High God, and He created us to work perfectly together in unity for His glory. Through Him, we *can* have a glorious marriage that is a testimony to Him. However, the enemy keeps us so at odds with each other that we have no concept of what God truly had in mind when He created us in His image!

Women have been so wrongly looked at and used throughout the countless generations since the fall in the garden. The world still misuses and abuses women—all the way from degrading them in movies, commercials, and pornography to sex trafficking, and everything in between. Women of all ages are depressed and live in a state of anxiety because they aren't skinny enough or pretty enough or young enough. We want straight hair when we have curly hair, we want to be skinny instead of embracing our curves, or we are too skinny and go to a doctor to "buy some curves." Women of all races and ages are confused and find it virtually impossible to find peace with who they are.

Many churches have taught for generations that women are to be seen and not heard. Many of us were taught that we needed to just tend the house and cook and clean. While there is absolutely nothing wrong with that role, it doesn't even come close to describing what God created us to be. I, for one, have been a stay-at-home wife and mother since my eldest son was born in December of 2000, and I am proud of that! I am a proud "keeper of my home" (Titus 2:5). But the world and the church both see that as "just" being a stay-at-home wife and mom. I've always taken my job very seriously, and yes, it is a job. Whether you stay at home or work outside the home, that is completely a nonissue in the meaning of our spiritual DNA.

I think we can all agree that everything God created has a purpose, right? (Sometimes I wonder about mosquitos and roaches, but let's stay focused.) God created all animals, birds, reptiles, insects, everything, and then said, "It is good." Then in Genesis 1:26–27, the Bible says, "And God said, 'Let Us make man in Our image, after Our likeness; and let them have dominion over the fish of the sea, and over the fowl of the air, and over the cattle, and over all the earth, and over every creeping thing that creepeth upon the earth.' So God created man in His own image, in the image of God created He him; male and female created He them" (emphasis mine).

Mankind, human beings, was the pinnacle of God's creation because we were created in *His* image. When God created mankind, He tucked the hidden gem of women right inside men. Adam was formed first, and Eve didn't come on the scene until Genesis 2:18. Eve was already there before she was ever fashioned. Basic knowledge of science tells us that within a man there are the X and Y chromosomes. Within a woman, there is XX. In every male, there is male and female, but women? Nope, we are XX. As my man likes to remind me often, "You were the crowning stroke, baby!" All women are the crowning stroke of God's creation. We truly are God's gift! Hang on, you'll see what I mean.

Genesis 2:18, in the King James Version, says, "It is not good that the man should be alone. I will make him an help meet for him."

Other translations describe *helpmeet* in these various ways:

- Helper, one who balances him—a counterpart who is suitable and complementary for him (AMP)
- Helper corresponding to him (CSB)
- A helper fit for him (ESV)
- A helper suitable for him (NIV)

No matter the translation you choose to read, the words *helpmeet* or *helper suitable* can't even come close to the original Hebrew meaning of those beautifully complex words. The Hebrew words for *helpmeet* are *ezer kenegdo*. Biblical scholars and experts in the Hebrew language all agree that these words are some of the most difficult to translate into the English language. Their meaning is so rich, which by the way, means *you* were made to be pretty amazing—the crowning stroke! The gift. Let's attempt to break this down:

> Ezer:
> to help, to surround, to protect or to aid

- It is a military term.
- The word *ezer* appears twenty-one times in the Old Testament and refers to military aid.
- Twice it is used for the woman.
- Three times for nations to whom Israel appealed for military aid.
- Sixteen times for *God* as Israel's helper and strength.

It is used consistently in a military context. David calls God his helper, his shield, and his defense. Do you see it? An ezer is a warrior!

Dr. Walter Bramson says this about the word *ezer*:

> When *Ezer* is examined in ancient Hebrew, a fascinating image appears. The ancient Hebrew letters were pictures that slowly evolved into the modern Hebrew letters used today. The ancient picture letters used for *Ezer* were an eye, a man, and a weapon! In other words, an *Ezer* is a revealer of man's enemy. *Ezer* is a mighty helper, a protector for her husband, and those in her influence.

Are there any Marvel comic movie fans reading this book? (Don't worry. I haven't forgotten what we're talking about. Give me a second for a very relevant rabbit trail here.)

I am a Marvel fan by default. I live in a household of men. I am always outnumbered when it comes to movie choices and then they beg me to stay and watch them with them. So I've come to like these movies. Until recently I couldn't say I had a favorite, not until I saw Black Panther! My men were shocked when I was so quickly drawn by this movie, and I could follow the storyline without asking a hundred questions. The thing that captured my attention most is that the warriors who surround the king of Wakanda, the ones who stand by at all times to protect him and to counsel him, are *women.* They are fierce. They are confident. And they take their roles very seriously. They are on the lookout for his enemies, and they are ready to fight for him and protect him. It's a beautiful example of what *ezer* means. Don't mess with my man in the spiritual *or* in the physical because I will go Wakanda on you.

Now let's take a look at the Hebrew word *kenegdo.* It means

> In front of (as in a mirror image),
> counterpart (corresponding to), so close
> in similarity so as to match or agree
> almost exactly

Let's put the two words together. *Ezer kenegdo* is a warrior of military strength who surrounds, protects, and comes to the aid of her husband. She is in front of him, as in a mirror image, so whatever move he makes, she is working with him like the image in the mirror. She corresponds so closely to him that they match and agree almost exactly. They work together like a well-oiled machine.

The enemy knew we, as women, were created to be a valuable asset to our men: a gift! He knew that if we knew our worth and what we were truly created to be, working together with our husbands, we would be unstoppable in the kingdom of God. This is why he came to Eve first instead of Adam. He came on the scene in Genesis 3 whispering his lies and twisting her thoughts away from what God had told her. When a woman doesn't know her real worth, the enemy is happy to bring in a lie that will redefine it for her. Lying is what our enemy does best.

The Hebrew word for *serpent* in Genesis 3 means "to hiss, to whisper, to prognosticate (or to prophesy)." He is a false prophet! John 8:44 calls him "the father of lies." He has been lying from the beginning. Ephesians 6:11 tells us to "put on the full armor of God so you can take your stand against the enemy's schemes." He plots and schemes against us to keep us from knowing our true value and worth as the image bearers and warriors of God.

Somewhere deep inside, women want to believe they are strong. We cling to any word of hope that we can be more than what we see ourselves to be. We flock to Bible studies, conferences, and personal growth studies by the thousands. We will even listen to secular women who seem to have it figured out if it will somehow motivate us to do something more. We don't need more motivation. We need inspiration given by *truth*. Eve was motivated to eat the fruit, but the motivation was a lie. The world can motivate, but only the Word of God can inspire and bring truth and show us who we really are.

Ladies, there is a strong warrior inside you, and her name is *Ezer*!

Questions for Thought

1. In what ways have you compared yourself to other women?
2. Have you felt inadequate?

3. Are you beginning to see how the enemy has lied to you in your own life?

Call to Action

Thank God for being your helper! Ask Him to reveal more truth to you as we continue in this book. Take the time to look up these verses and meditate on God as your helper: Psalm 10:14, Psalm 30:10, Psalm 33:20, Psalm 42:5, Psalm 46:1, and Psalm 54:4.

Chapter 5

Warriors Know Their Enemy

Warriors are not always the fastest or strongest people.
Strength and speed can be developed through training.
Warriors are those who choose to stand between their
enemy and all that they love and hold sacred.

—Unknown

So why did Adam need a helpmeet? I've heard it said, and I must agree loudly that Adam needed a helper suitable for him because there was an enemy in the garden and he could not stand against him alone.

Will you stay with me for a moment of exegesis? Don't know what exegesis means? That's okay, most people don't, and neither did I until someone told me once that I exegete the Scriptures well. So being the student of the Bible that I am, I had to go look that up.

Exegesis: critical explanation or interpretation of a text, especially of scripture.

Notice it's a critical explanation. What we are about to discover is critical. Now with that definition in mind, let's exegete some things.

First, let's paint a picture here. Satan, the enemy that was in the garden, was *not* what we picture him being. We imagine that he must've been snakelike because the Bible refers to him as a "serpent" in Genesis 3. As we've already seen, *serpent* in Hebrew means "to hiss, to whisper, to prognosticate." *Prognosticate* means "to prophecy." He was and still is a false prophet that whispers lies. He was *not* a snake hanging from a tree with an apple curled up in his tail waving it in front of Eve. He was not and is not some scary-looking creature that we might see in a horror movie. He does not wear a red suit with horns, a pointy tail, and a pitchfork. In fact, in Ezekiel 28 the Bible tells us that when he was created he was an angel that was the "model of perfection, full of wisdom, and perfect in beauty." His very being consisted of beautiful precious stones. Ezekiel 28:13 says he was "in Eden, the garden of God." So when he approached Eve, he wasn't scary to her at all. The garden was paradise. They didn't even know what it meant to have an enemy yet. Not until he deceived them.

Ezekiel 28:14 says that he was "anointed as a guardian cherub…he was on the holy mount of God…he walked among the fiery stones." The Hebrew word *anointed* here means "consecrated."

Consecrated means "dedicated for a divine purpose." Before he was tossed out of heaven, Lucifer had been created for a divine purpose. Ezekiel 28:14 goes on to say he was anointed as a "guardian cherub" or "cherub that covereth" in the King James. The word *covereth* here in Hebrew means "to fence in, cover over, protect, defend, or hedge in." Sound familiar? Remember an ezer is a helper, a surrounding, and protecting aid of military strength. The meanings are very similar, wouldn't you agree?

Let's continue to exegete.

Verse 14 says that he "walked up and down in the midst of the stones of fire." The word *stones* in Hebrew means "to build."

Let's put these puzzle pieces together by inserting Proverbs 14:1, "A wise woman builds her home, but a foolish woman tears it down with her own hands." The word *build* here is the same word as the word for *stones* in Ezekiel 28:14. Lucifer had been divinely created for the purpose of building a defense around the very Mountain of God. Ezekiel 28:14 says he was "on the Holy Mountain of God" until wickedness was found in him. When God created man and woman in His image, the enemy recognized something in Eve. Something that looked strangely close to what his job had been on the Mountain of God. She had a unique DNA and beauty, a glory that would reflect and bring honor to the Father, and that was the very thing the enemy wanted for himself.

He wanted the worship that the Most High received. He wanted to ascend to the throne. He recognized that if Adam and Eve used the spiritual DNA that was in them, together they would be unstoppable. So he approached Ezer, the one who was meant to be so fierce in her surrounding protection and help that she would be as fierce as an army of men. (Oh, girls, we are going to get to *that* in the next chapter! You are a force to be reckoned with, an army of one, but wait, I can't jump ahead.) He knew if he could keep her from reflecting her part of the image of the Almighty that in turn, it would keep Adam from being the valiant image bearer God created him to be. If he could stop her, he could stop them.

God's original design for us, as man and woman, was to work together, not against each other. One of the Hebrew words for *man* is *geh`-ber*, and it means "to be strong, to prevail, be valiant, warrior." For the man to fully rise to this call, God created an ezer for him, one who was made to come alongside him and surround and protect him so that he could prevail. Man and woman were made to be the original "world powers" that join together to take down evil, but we fell for a lie.

The enemy didn't have to do great feats to get them to fall into sin. He simply had to make them question God. He used one little seed of doubt, "did God really say," to go after the seed that was to come from the union of Adam and Eve. That seed would be our Lord and Savior Jesus Christ.

Genesis 3:15 tells us that the enemy would bruise the heel of this seed but that this seed would then crush the enemy's head. The work of dispelling the lie began and is still ongoing. I believe that the Spirit of the living God is moving in our time to raise up generations of men and women who know how to fight the *real* enemy. God has placed a seed in each of us that is God's intended purpose and calling on our lives, and the enemy is still whispering lies, falsely prophesying over us to keep us from that intended purpose. He still tries to bruise the heels of the followers of Christ, but that's all he can do. As individuals and as covenant partners in marriage, there are seeds in us, seeds of eternal purpose. We must not allow the enemy to lie to us any longer. Truth dispels lies, and it silences the prognosticator.

Questions for Thought

1. Have you and your husband been treating each other as enemies?
2. Have you heard the whispers of the prognosticator? What are some of the lies he's had you believing?
3. Discuss how you feel about being called "God's gift" as it relates to this chapter.

Call to Action

Pray and ask God to help you and your husband to see each other the way God sees you. Ask him to help you learn how to fight the real enemy and not each other. Ask Him to help you become unstoppable for the kingdom of God.

Chapter 6

An Army of One

> Who can find a virtuous woman? For
> her price is far above rubies.
>
> —Proverbs 31:10

Proverbs 31—as women, this chapter of the Bible usually makes us cringe a little inside. It brings to the forefront what's always lingering in the back of our minds, "I'll never be enough."

"I just can't do it all."

"I'm not worthy to be his wife."

"My kids would be better off with a different mom."

"I'm just not worthy."

"Everyone else has it all together, but I'm a hot mess!"

Reading about the Proverbs 31 woman makes us feel like we can never measure up to this and that surely this woman never really existed. Maybe she did, and maybe she didn't, but either way, I want us to take a different look at this. All from the vantage point of verse 10, "Who can find a virtuous woman? For her price is far above rubies."

Since we're on a roll in exegeting scripture, let's just keep rolling, shall we?

According to the dictionary the word *virtuous* means "having or showing high moral standards." It makes most of us squirm because we feel that our life is anything but virtuous, especially if people knew our past, right? We don't want anyone to open our closet of skeletons. Virtuous? No, most of us feel as far from virtuous as we can get. We don't feel worthy. Sure, we try to live right and do good, but virtuous? No.

But what does virtuous mean in Hebrew? It's altogether different and superbly spectacular, and it puts all of us girls on a level playing field.

> Virtuous: A force, an army, valor, strength, band of soldiers, a great company, might, power, riches, worthy.

"Hold on, Michelle, where's the level playing field here, because I don't feel like any of that."

Hold that thought and stay with me. This word stems from a root word in Hebrew that means "twist or whirl, to dance or writhe in pain (wait, what?), to wait, to bring forth, grieve, stay, tarry, travail with pain, tremble, trust, wait carefully, be wounded." *Whoa*! The field just leveled. Whether you see someone else's pain or not, we can all identify with the root part of this word.

I know that's a lot to take in, so let's digest this. This word is like our words in English which are called compound words. To fully understand the whole word, you must understand the root word first. To get to the part of virtuous that says "we are so strong that we are a force like an army of men," we must first go through some pain. Just like being pregnant, you must go through pain before you get the sweetness of the baby. Many women have experienced pain in their lives far too early. It has shaped who they are and makes them fertile ground for the lies of the enemy. Others have to live a little life before they realize that it's hard, and yet they are still fertile ground for the lies of the enemy. Our enemy doesn't want us to know that our God will use our pain, our waiting, our grieving, and our trusting to make us such a force that the enemy will never want to reckon with us again.

Here is the superbly spectacular part of this Hebrew word. It is only ever used in the Old Testament to describe a woman. It was used by Boaz to describe Ruth in the book that bears her name in chapter 3, verse 11. In Proverbs 12:4, we read, "A virtuous woman is a crown to her husband, but she who causes shame is like rottenness in his bones." (*Yikes!* I want to stay on the front end of that verse.) Then at the end of Proverbs 31, in verse 29, we see it again: "Many daughters have done virtuously, but thou excellest them all."

Isn't this extraordinary? Our God uses the word *virtuous* to describe a woman who has come through some agonizing pain but has come out on the other side stronger because of it. This isn't a woman who has come through pain with a hardened heart, callous, and cynical toward others. This describes a virtue that can only be obtained through complete dependence on Jesus Himself.

When we allow Him to take us through thick darkness where all we feel is fear and we see no way out, something begins to shift in the Spirit. When we are filled with questions and anxiety, yet we cry out to Him for help, trusting in His goodness, we find strength we didn't know we could possess. When we praise Him and worship Him instead of complaining and worrying, the demons of hell start to tremble in fear. Virtue begins to form in us like muscles on a bodybuilder. The enemy no longer sees a weak woman that he can push around and lie to. My friend, he sees an ezer! He sees an army, an army of *one* that has the strength of one thousand. We are like a Holy Spirit-filled she-hulk in the spirit!

Eleanor Roosevelt said, "A woman is like a tea bag. You never know how strong she is until you put her in hot water." I doubt Mrs. Roosevelt knew she had just summed up the Hebrew definition of the word *virtuous*.

This sounds amazing, and maybe you even feel pumped up, but fleshing this out is hard. It goes beyond calling it work. This is a straight-up war, and no war is ever won without a fierce battle. No soldier is ever sent into battle without first being trained on how to fight and informed about the enemy. For the most part, our modern Christian culture has failed miserably at training us on how to fight spiritual warfare. As for being informed about our enemy and knowing his strategies, just take a look around to see how many of the people you know who truly walk in victory. I can almost see the look on your face as you're thinking, "Not many." Yep, me too.

Oh, but my friend, I believe God is sending out a message to His girls that will equip us to be victorious and to help lead others to that same victory. We have to know what He put in us. We are warriors, girls. We are fierce! We have the strength of an army of men in us. Oh, and did you catch the last word of the definition of *virtuous*? Worthy. Oh, sister, close your eyes. Take in a deep breath. He calls you worthy.

> The King is enthralled by your beauty; honor Him, for He is your Lord. (Psalm 45:11)

Questions for Thought

1. How have you felt reading about the Proverbs 31 woman in the past?

2. Do you see it differently now?
3. As you feel led, share with each other some of the painful parts of your life and how God was faithful to you through it.
4. Did you ever imagine that through your pain, God was making you into a virtuous woman, an army of one?

Call to Action

Let the chapter cause you to worship our amazing God. Worship Him for His goodness and His faithfulness in your life. Thank Him for using the most agonizing times in your life to make you so fierce that the enemy thinks twice before messing with you again. Just lift your hands and voices right where you are. Oh, praise the name of the Lord our God!

Chapter 7

You Are Marked

Now that we've learned that God gave us a spiritual DNA that we never knew we had, and now that we've learned that we are an army of one, I want to take us deeper. Everything we've learned so far is crucial to us in knowing the strength and power we possess as women of God. These are not just words to read and forget. These truths need to go deep. Grasp on to them. Cling to them. Ask the Lord to let this sink deeply into your spirit. Ask Him to help you implement this daily as you learn how to become the ezer He made you to be. Implementing it daily is like daily workouts that make you stronger and stronger a little at a time. You don't make your goals overnight. You grow little by little. I've heard it said that we are not changed by the words we hear but by the words we apply. James 1:22 says, "Do not merely listen to the word, and so deceive yourselves. Do what it says." In this case, you won't be changed merely by reading the words of this book. You must appropriate them and apply them.

In Ephesians 1:13–14, we read, "In Him you also trusted, after you heard the word of truth, the gospel of your salvation; in whom also, having believed, you were sealed with the Holy Spirit of promise, who is the guarantee of our inheritance until the redemption of the purchased possession, to the praise of His glory."

The word for *sealed* in this verse in the Greek is awesome. It means "to fence in, block up, protection from misappropriation, to stop." In ancient times, a king's signet ring was used to seal documents. It could not be tampered with, and even the king himself could not revoke what had been written in the document once the seal was applied. It was protected from misappropriation.

In Scripture, a seal represents three things:

1. A finished transaction. From the cross Jesus said, "It is finished" (John 19:30). John 17:4 says, "I have brought you glory on earth by completing the work you gave me to do."
2. A sign of ownership. 2 Timothy 2:19a says, "Nevertheless, God's solid foundation stands firm, sealed with this inscription: 'The Lord knows those who are His.'" God knows those who belong to Him. His sign of ownership is on us!
3. Security. "Now write another decree in the king's name in behalf of the Jews as seems best to you, and seal it with the king's signet ring—for no document written in the king's name and sealed with his ring can be revoked" (Esther 8:8). "A stone was brought and placed over the mouth of the den, and the king sealed it with his own signet ring and with the rings of his nobles, so that Daniel's situation might not be changed" (Daniel 6:17). "And do not grieve the Holy Spirit of God, with whom you were sealed for the day of redemption" (Ephesians 4:30).

We can clearly see that if we have accepted Jesus as our Lord and Savior, we have been sealed by God. The Holy Spirit is the King of king's signet seal on us. We are marked! In the spirit realm, that mark is clearly seen. The enemy of our souls sees it. Just imagine what that looks like. It may say something like, "Property of the King of kings." When the enemy sees that, he knows he can't mess with you. He knows you are fenced about by the hosts of heaven. He knows you are protected from misappropriation. He will do everything in his power to make you forget this, but that doesn't change the fact that you are sealed. Jesus paid the price for us on the cross. The transaction was completed. His seal of ownership was placed on us and we are secure. Nothing can ever revoke it.

Now it's time to wrap this thing up and put a giant mind-blowing bow on it. Maybe I should say a big Hebrew bow. Either way, you're going to love this. As we've already established, the Hebrew language is so rich. The Greek is as well.

Just a sidebar for those who do not know, the Old Testament was written in Hebrew, and the New Testament was written in Greek and Aramaic. Our English just cannot compare.

The Hebrew is especially rich. Even the individual letters have significance. Let's focus on the Hebrew letter shin.

The shin is the twenty-first letter of the Hebrew alphabet. Many important Hebrew words have this letter in their spelling. For instance, in the word *Jerusalem*, or *Yerushalayim*, the shin appears in the middle of the word. It is also in the middle of *Yeshua*, the Hebrew name of our Savior. It is also in *El Shaddai*. The shin is actually the first letter of *Shaddai*. It is seen as the initial of Almighty *El Shaddai*.

Jews worldwide place what is called a mezuzah on their doorposts.

Inside contains a small hand-written parchment scroll with these verses on it in Hebrew:

> Hear, O Israel: The Lord our God,
> the Lord is one. Love the Lord your God
> with all your heart and with all your soul
> and with all your strength. These com-
> mandments that I give you today are to
> be on your hearts. Impress them on your
> children. Talk about them when you sit at
> home and when you walk along the road,
> when you lie down and when you get
> up. Tie them as symbols on your hands

and bind them on your foreheads. Write them on the doorframes of your houses and on your gates. (Deuteronomy 6:4–9)

It is a land the Lord your God cares for; the eyes of the Lord your God are continually on it from the beginning of the year to its end. So if you faithfully obey the commands I am giving you today—to love the Lord your God and to serve him with all your heart and with all your soul—then I will send rain on your land in its season, both autumn and spring rains, so that you may gather in your grain, new wine and olive oil. I will provide grass in the fields for your cattle, and you will eat and be satisfied. Be careful, or you will be enticed to turn away and worship other gods and bow down to them. Then the Lord's anger will burn against you, and he will shut up the heavens so that it will not rain and the ground will yield no produce, and you will soon perish from the good land the Lord is giving you. Fix these words of mine in your hearts and minds; tie them as symbols on your hands and bind them on your foreheads. Teach them to your children, talking about them when you sit at home and when you walk along the road, when you lie down and when you get up. Write them on the doorframes of your houses and on your gates, so that your days and the days of your children

may be many in the land the Lord swore
to give your ancestors, as many as the
days that the heavens are above the earth.
(Deuteronomy 11:12–21)

On every mezuzah, the shin is at the top. It signifies that *El Shaddai* is "The Almighty—the Guardian of Israel's doors" and that He protects this family. It bears the initial of His name.

In 2 Chronicles 6:6, it says, "But now I have chosen Jerusalem for my *name* to be there, and I have chosen David to rule my people Israel" (emphasis mine). The city of Jerusalem is built over three valleys: the Hinnom Valley, the Tyropean (or central) Valley, and the Kidron Valley. God instructed David to build his capitol city in Jerusalem and King Solomon to build His temple there, because He had chosen Jerusalem to put His name there. When you do an aerial view over the city of Jerusalem, you see the shin.

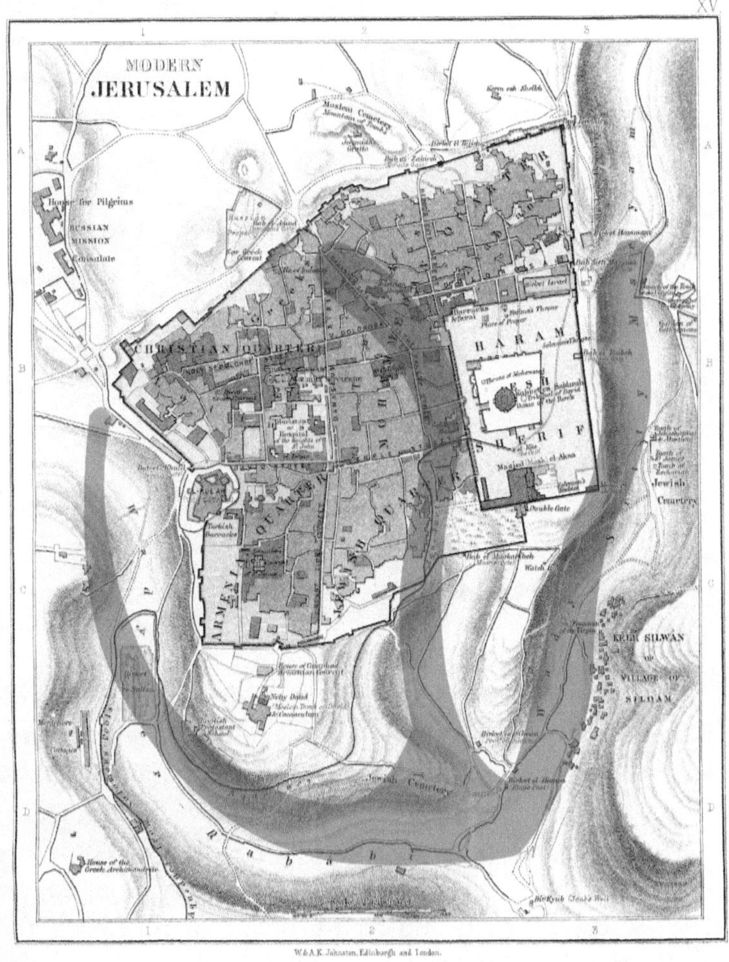

When God said He had chosen Jerusalem for His name to be there, He meant it! Jerusalem sits on top of the name of the Almighty *El Shaddai*.

Let's get to the mind-blowing bow to wrap this up. Ecclesiastes 3:11 tells us, "He has made everything beautiful in its time. He has also set eternity in the human heart; yet, no one can fathom what God has done from beginning to end." When the human heart is split in half, this is what we see.

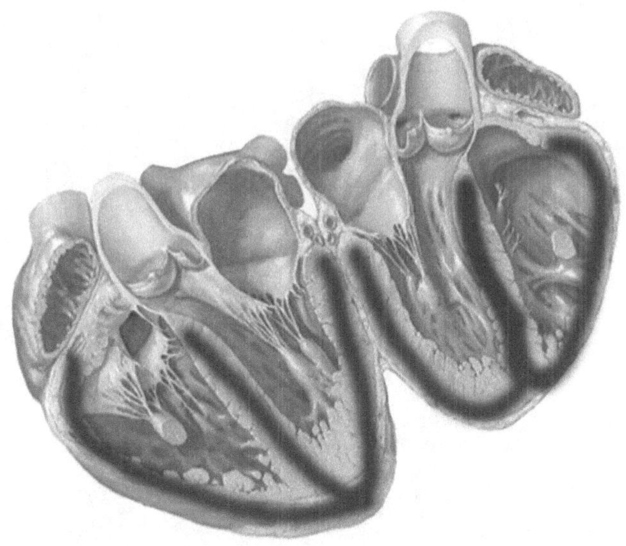

Even down to our very biological anatomy, God placed His name on us. He set eternity in the hearts of all mankind, even those who would reject Him. Daniel 9:18b–19 says, "We do not make requests of you because we are righteous, but because of Your great mercy. O Lord, listen! O Lord, forgive! O Lord, hear and act! For Your sake, O my God, do not delay, because Your city and Your people bear Your Name."

Ezers, when life is coming hard at you and the enemy's voice is loud and obnoxious, remind him whose name you bear. When he tells you that your marriage can never be salvaged, you remind him that you are a warrior all the way down to your DNA and that you will not surrender to him. When he tells you that you aren't good enough and you'll never measure up, tell him that you were bought by the blood of Jesus and that you've been sealed by His Holy Spirit. Remind him you are protected from misappropriation. Remind him he's already defeated. Remind him he is under your feet. Then tell him to take a hike.

> For this reason I kneel before the Father, from whom every family in heaven and on earth derives its name. I pray that out of his glorious riches he may strengthen you with power through his Spirit in your inner being, so that Christ may dwell in your hearts through faith. And I pray that you, being rooted and established in love, may have power, together with all the Lord's holy people, to grasp how wide and long and high and deep is the love of Christ, and to know this love that surpasses knowledge—that you may be filled to the measure of all the fullness of God. Now to him who is able to do immeasurably more than all we ask or imagine, according to his power that is at work within us, to him be glory in the church and in Christ Jesus throughout all generations, for ever and ever! Amen. (Ephesians 3:14–21)

Questions for Thought

1. This chapter was loaded. Go back and discuss the beauty of the truth that you are sealed by the Holy Spirit and all that this means.
2. Take time to go back over the scriptures that reveal the very initial of the Almighty *El Shaddai.*

Call to Action

Pray and ask the Lord to help these truths to be engraved deeply in your spirit. We so easily forget. Ask the Lord to remind you every time you feel defeated that you are protected from misappropriation and that you bear the name of *El Shaddai.*

Chapter 8

Ezers Don't Run From Giants

Life's giants before you are ants to God. God is
in you so face your giants. Let them fall on their
faces. Pray to slay. You are a giant slayer.

—Ceo Isaac

Face the giants in your life, slay them and move on. Do
not be daunted by the mistakes and failures in your life.

—T. D. Jakes

May I have a moment of vulnerability here? When the Lord
revealed the truth of what He put inside of each woman's
spiritual DNA, my mind was blown! I felt fierce and strong
like I could kick Satan's teeth in. But the fact of the matter is,
I don't feel that way most of the time. It is a daily intentional
battle to remind myself that I am an ezer. Life's giants taunt
us endlessly like Goliath taunted the Israelites in 1 Samuel
17. Goliath would come out every day for forty days, from
sunrise to sunset and mock the Israelites and their God. Isn't
that just how the enemy works? He starts mocking us and

making us question our God from the moment we wake until we go to bed. His goal is to defeat us before we ever put our feet on the floor and continue till we go to bed so that we have sleepless nights of tossing and turning.

Here's my vulnerable moment: this book has been my giant. I made a bold announcement in front of a lot of people back in 2018 that I was going to write this book. From that statement, a giant arose, and he has come out daily to taunt me and tell me I can't do this. The first mocking statement this giant threw at me was telling me that putting our story of dealing with pornography and the other things we've been through in print would be a bad idea. Sure, I had shared our story on our ministry social media forum, but it's a private group. Certain people's names and faces floated before me that I felt would be judgmental and condemning, and I just wanted to shrink back. Then God gave me a stone to hurl at the giant through my husband.

I told Brian my fears, and he told me that I was listening to lies and that our story needed to be shared. I took a deep breath and moved forward. The next taunt from the giant was to make me question if anyone would even want to read the book. What if it was a colossal flop? What if only my family and friends bought one? I would look so foolish. What credibility do I have to write a book? Since I'm being vulnerable anyway, let me keep it real. As I type these words, those questions still loom large, but I ran across this quote today by Hudson Taylor: "All God's giants have been weak men and women who have gotten hold of God's faithfulness."

This was another God-given stone in my pouch to hurl back at this giant. It was a reminder to me today that I am one of God's giants. Glory to His mighty name! I am one of His ezers, and so are you. Whatever God says we can do, we can do it. Whatever God calls us to do, He equips us for it.

The giants we see in our lives are like ants to God. We are ezer giant slayers. Ezers don't run from giants.

All our giants look different. Some come in the form of anxiety, depression, addiction, self-image, fear of the future, guilt from the past, being overwhelmed, and feeling we aren't enough. Others come in the form of words said about us in our past—*stupid, ugly, fat, worthless, not talented, can't do anything right*, etc. Still, others hover over us through our perceived failures: loss of a job, divorce, lost dreams, wayward children, estranged relationships with family, and debt.

We could go on and on naming one giant after another. The common thread in every giant we will ever face is *fear*. We have all heard the saying "Fear is a liar." Let's make this even plainer by looking at the word *FEAR* as an acrostic:

F—False
E—Evidence
A—Appearing
R—Real

Satan uses fear in our lives to put a choke hold on us. It strangles us as one fear leads to another and another, and soon fear is all around us. It spreads like kudzu. If you aren't familiar with kudzu, it is a rampant growing vine that covers and takes over everything around it. It grows up and out and spreads everywhere. Here where I live, we see it everywhere.

Not long ago, Brian and I passed a little house that was almost entirely covered in kudzu. You could see that at one time this little house was adorable but had somehow been abandoned, and the unkept yard was taken over by the kudzu. The kudzu then started taking over the house, and all you could see that was left of the house was the little front porch. The house was still there. It was just engulfed in the kudzu, and pretty soon, no one would even know that,

that little house was underneath all that mess. This is what false evidence appearing real does to us. At one time, that little house was built by someone with hopes and dreams of a family that would love and laugh and make memories in it. Much the same way our Creator, God, made us with specific purposes for His glory.

Jeremiah 29:11 says He has plans for us, to prosper us, and not to harm us. However, all the giants in our lives come to plant the kudzu of fear, and it spreads and strangles our lives. Soon, all the God-given hopes, dreams, and purposes He has planned for us get covered, and we don't even recognize ourselves anymore. We don't see how God could even love us, let alone use us for His glory. False evidence appearing real has taken over.

This is just what happened in Numbers 13. God tells Moses to send some men into Canaan to explore it. He said to Moses in verse 1, "Send some men to explore the land of Canaan, which I am giving to the Israelites." God had a special gift that He was giving to the Israelites, and just like my daddy when he's excited to give us gifts, He couldn't wait for them to see it. So He tells Moses to send some guys in to explore it and come back and tell everyone all about it.

Moses picks his men, one from each of the twelve tribes. He gives them specific instructions to see what the land is like and whether the people there are strong or weak, few or many. Is the land good or bad? Is it unwalled or fortified? Is the soil fertile? Are there trees? Oh, and bring back some fruit.

With marching orders in hand, the twelve men set out on their exploration expedition. Verse 23 tells us that when they reached the Valley of Eshcol, they cut off a branch bearing a single cluster of grapes. Two of the men had to carry the cluster on a pole between them. It also adds that they threw some pomegranates and figs on the pole too. Now I don't know about you, but I haven't had to put any poles in my car lately to bring my fruit home from the produce section. This land was rockin'. I would say the soil was very fertile. I can just picture the Lord as He watches their faces when they see these grapes. It's like watching your little ones open their gifts at Christmas, and you sit back and soak in their glee.

These dudes snoop around for forty days and then return to give their report to Moses. After reading about those grapes and seeing that they hung out for forty days, you would think they would come back with a unanimously cheerful report. You would think that on their travels back to their people that they would have all discussed their thoughts and been on the same page with their findings; however, that is not what we read next. Verse 27 tells us they said, "We went into the land to which you sent us, and it does flow with milk and honey. Here is the fruit." Then verse 28 starts with *but*. Girls, we have to watch our buts.

"I know God's Word is true and I believe it, but…"

"I know the Word says I'm an overcomer and that I'm victorious, but…"

"I know I shouldn't worry, but…"

Our buts get us in trouble.

The explorers then begin to describe the people who lived there. They describe them as powerful. They describe the cities as fortified and very large. As they are spreading their fear tactics, one of the twelve, Caleb, just can't take it anymore. He silences the people and says, "We can take these people! We can do this!" But the other men wouldn't hear of it. They said the people of the land were stronger and that the land devoured those living in it. They said the people living there were giants and that they seemed like grasshoppers in comparison. The Bible says they spread a bad report among the Israelites. *Wow*, this sounds curiously similar to our world today when you turn on the news or look at social media.

Who am I kidding? We don't even have to turn on the news; this is what happens in our heads every day! False evidence appearing real.

In Numbers 14, we continue to read that this bad report caused such a stink that all the people wailed and carried on asking Moses why he had brought them out of Egypt. Why didn't he just leave them there? Surely, they would've been better off. This grieved Moses and Aaron so much that they fell on their faces before the Lord. While they were weeping and praying, Caleb and Joshua were still out among all the naysayers. They tore their clothes and said, "This land is exceedingly good! If the Lord is pleased with us, He will lead us into it. It's a land that flows with milk and honey and He will give it to us! Only we cannot rebel against Him." I love this next part: "Do not be afraid of the people of the land, because we will swallow them up. Their protection is gone, but the Lord is with us. Do not be afraid of them." The fear-mongers would not listen, and they started talking of stoning them.

Then the glory of the Lord appeared at the Tent of Meeting to all the Israelites. God had had enough. He didn't just show up to Moses and Aaron who were praying, He appeared to *all* the Israelites. He was ready to wipe them all out and start over. Moses began reminding God that His protection of His people was known to other nations. If He wiped them out, what would the other nations think about Him then? He reminded God of all He had done for the Israelites in the past. Then Moses comes in with the icing on the cake. He says in chapter 14:17–19,

> Now may the Lord's strength be dis-
> played, just as You have declared: "The
> Lord is slow to anger, abounding in love
> and forgiving sin and rebellion. Yet He

> does not leave the guilty unpunished; he
> punishes the children for the sin of the
> fathers to the third and fourth genera-
> tion." In accordance with Your great love,
> forgive the sin of these people, just as You
> have pardoned them from the time they
> left Egypt until now.

God relents and decides to forgive the Israelites; how-ever, you must pay attention to the next part. There would be consequences. God told them that not one of the men who saw His glory and miraculous signs in Egypt would get to see the promised land. Their lack of faith led to fear, and their fear led to grumbling against the Lord. False evidence appearing real, left unchecked like the kudzu, will cause us to lose sight of all God has done for us in the past. Fueled fear causes us to forget His faithfulness. Lack of faith in itself isn't the problem. We all face times when our faith gets weak.

In 2 Timothy 2:13, it says, "If we are faithless, He will remain faithful, for He cannot disown Himself." My sister ezer, Jesus is faithfulness itself. Just look at Revelation 19:11, "I saw heaven standing open and there before me was a white horse, whose rider is called Faithful and True." When the Word tells us He cannot disown Himself, it is because *His name is faithful.* Oh, my sister, He will never condemn you for weak faith. His name will carry you. The problem comes in when we feed our lack of faith and let it turn to fear that obscures the truth of His faithfulness. The enemy comes in and robs us of our promises. We miss the beauty of what God has for us on the other side of those giants that loom over us.

Pastor Steven Furtick says this, "Don't get so over-whelmed by what you're walking into that you forget who you're walking in with."

Now, sisters, *that* will preach! As ezers, we are image bearers of the Most High God, our King. According to Jesus's own words in Luke 10:19, we have "been given authority to overcome all the power of the enemy." It also says nothing will harm us. The giants of a struggling marriage, divorce, wayward children, singleness, loneliness, depression, anxiety, financial issues, past sexual abuse, and pornography all have to bow down to the name that is above every other name. That name is written all over your spiritual DNA.

Bring the King with you onto the battlefield where you fight your giants and in His name remind those giants about your DNA. Where is the battlefield? We talked about it at the beginning of this book. It is in prayer. When you pray, tell the enemy that an ezer has shown up.

There is one last quote I want to share with you in this chapter. The author of this quote is unknown:

> There are two possible attitudes
> when facing a giant. One is to say, "It's so
> big there's nothing I can do." The other is
> to say, "It's so big I can't miss it!"

Girls, if God is for us, who can be against us? Take that giant down!

Questions for Thought

1. What have been some of your giants in life?
2. What things do you now see as False Evidence Appearing Real?
3. What "kudzu" have you allowed to choke things in your life?
4. The Lord doesn't condemn us for small faith, but it does say He is pleased with big faith. The Word

never tells us that we can have too much faith. Discuss that. Great faith pleases God.

Call to Action

Get alone with God and ask Him for strength to slay your giants. Ask Him to help you have great faith. Ask Him to reveal to you the things in life that are False Evidence Appearing Real. Use the Word of God as your spiritual weed killer and start getting rid of the kudzu.

Chapter 9

Keep Pouring

I recently watched a podcast called "Marriage Be Hard." I laughed at the name and thought to myself, *Yep. It be hard sometimes!* In fact, life is just hard. Jesus said in John 10 that He came to give us life and that we might have it more abundantly. He also said that in this world, we would have tribulation. He ended that statement with, "Take heart. I have overcome the world." He knew that life and married life would be hard, but He called us to have courage. Just because life is hard doesn't mean that it isn't also precious and filled with blessings everywhere. And just because marriage "be hard" doesn't mean it can't still be glorious.

The hard times in life and in marriage often leave us broken and hopeless. We see our circumstances like a shattered piece of glass in a thousand tiny pieces that can never be put back together again. How can we possibly be an ezer to anyone? How can we be strong and slay giants when everywhere we look we only see brokenness?

God looks at our brokenness sort of like the Japanese art of *kintsugi*, the art of precious scars. This is the art of taking broken bowls, teapots, or some precious vase that is in a thousand pieces and repairing them in such a way that highlights and enhances the brokenness thus adding great value to the piece. *Kintsugi* literally means "golden repair." This traditional Japanese art uses precious metal such as liquid gold, liquid silver, or lacquer dusted with powdered gold to bring together the broken pieces while at the same time enhancing the brokenness.

One article on this art form from Lifegate.com puts it this way,

> The technique consists in joining fragments and giving them a new, more refined aspect. Every repaired piece is unique, because of the randomness with which ceramic shatters and the irregular patterns formed that are enhanced with the use of metals. With this technique it's possible to create true and always different works of art, each with its own story and beauty, thanks to the unique cracks formed when the object breaks, as if they were wounds that leave different marks on each of us.

This makes me think of the song "Thankful for the Scars" by I Am They.

> Waking up to a new sunrise
> Looking back from the other side
> I can see now with open eyes
> Darkest water and deepest pain
> I wouldn't trade it for anything
> 'Cause my brokenness brought me to you
> And these wounds are a story you'll use
> So I'm thankful for the scars

'Cause without them I wouldn't know
    your heart
And I know they'll always tell of who you
    are
So forever I am thankful for the scars
Now I'm standing in confidence
With the strength of your faithfulness
And I'm not who I was before
No, I don't have to fear anymore
So I'm thankful for the scars
'Cause without them I wouldn't know
    your heart
And I know they'll always tell of who you
    are
So forever I am thankful for the scars
I can see, I can see
How you delivered me
In your hands, in your feet
I found my victory
I'm thankful for your scars
'Cause without them I wouldn't know
    your heart
And with my life, I'll tell of who you are
So forever I am thankful
I'm thankful for the scars
'Cause without them I wouldn't know
    your heart
And I know they'll always tell of who you
    are
So forever I am thankful for the scars

Our brokenness brings us to Jesus. Just as kintsugi uses precious metals to repair and bring value, His precious blood and divine purposes repairs us and brings beauty from our brokenness.

The Bible is replete with redemptive stories of brokenness, but I just want to focus on one of them. In 2 Kings 4:1–7, it tells us of a widow whose husband was "of the sons of the prophets." He left her and their two boys with debt, and now his creditor was coming after her for what was owed. He wanted to take her two sons as his slaves. She came to the prophet Elisha for help. It is clear from the scripture that her husband has some affiliation with the prophets. Some think he was literally the son of a prophet, and some believe this to mean that he was a student of the prophets. Either way, she knew who to go to for help. Elisha says to her in verse 2, "Tell me, what do you have in *your house*?" (emphasis mine). Her reply was, "Your servant has nothing there at all, just a little oil." Elisha tells her to go around and ask all her neighbors for empty jars, and he follows up his instruction by saying, "Don't ask for just a few." He then instructs her to go inside and shut the door behind her and her sons, then pour oil into all the jars, and as each was filled she was to put them to the side.

I'm sure all this seemed odd to the woman. Here she was a widow, broken by sorrow and filled with fear of her sons being taken as slaves to pay their father's debt. She was broken and desperate. The prophet asked what she had in her house. If I could get in her head, I think she might have been thinking, "If I had anything in my house I would have given it to the creditor already to pay the debt. What do I have? I have nothing but this oil and that won't help a thing!"

As crazy as it sounds, Elisha was telling her to focus on what she did have, rather than what she didn't. The solution to her problem was going to come out of what seemed like her lack. The answer was going to come from her brokenness. Isn't it just like God commanding us to do what we are certain we cannot do? We see our broken pieces, and we are certain they can never be put back together again. We see our broken marriage and believe that it is unsalvageable. Then God asks us to forgive. He asks us to show kindness when none is shown to us. He asks us to give respect when we feel it hasn't been earned. God looks at us and asks us what we have in "our house."

What do you have left in you to give? Our response? Nothing! I have nothing else to give. I have a weary, beaten-up, broken heart. That's it. That's all I have. And God says, "I can work with that." He wants you to come and ask Him to help you as you pour out from your brokenness. Just like He instructed the widow to go ask all her neighbors for jars and don't ask for just a few, He wants you to come to Him with great expectation of what He will do with your broken pieces.

The next part of the instruction is interesting. He tells her to take the jars home and shut the door behind her and her sons and then pour the oil and keep pouring. Why would he tell her that detailed instruction? It is because of what we do in private that causes us to be able to keep pouring. There is no way in our human frailty that we can forgive, show kindness, serve, or give respect when we are so broken that we can barely breathe, let alone pour into someone who caused our brokenness to begin with. Maybe your brokenness comes from something else in life. Maybe you aren't married but you've been broken by other circumstances, and God is asking you to pour out and serve others when all you want to do is stay in bed and never get up again.

Pouring from your own emptiness is the last thing you want to do. In our own strength we cannot do any of this. It's what we do when we shut the door behind us. We can choose to shut the door and crawl into bed and binge-watch Netflix and eat carbs, or we can choose to get alone with Jesus and let

Him pour into us. When we do this, something supernatural begins to happen. When the widow obeyed the prophet, her little bit of oil kept flowing. Every time she turned it up to fill another jar, miraculously there was more oil. The prophet had given her the solution to her problem. It was how she would pay her husband's creditors.

The same will happen for us when we pour out of the little we have in "our house." It's miraculous. Supernatural.

He whispers to the ezer in us and tells us that we are strong because it's in our spiritual DNA. He tells us that we are beautiful and glorious. He tells us He knows us and He sees us. He tells us that He goes before us and He is our rear guard. He tells us that He alone can put in us the desire to do what seems impossible and pour out of our brokenness. He tells us that while we are obeying, He is working on our behalf in ways we cannot see. When we emerge from behind the shut door, we find a strength we didn't know we possessed. As we obey and pour out the forgiveness or give the respect and keep pouring, we find that something beautiful is happening. "Keep pouring" are the operative words here. We can't try to forgive and then take it back. We can't try to be kind, and then when it isn't reciprocated right away, say we knew it wouldn't work. We must keep pouring. When we keep pouring, our broken pieces suddenly start to come together, and in spite of the scars, something beautiful starts to form.

Remember the kintsugi art and the quote from Lifegate?

> Every repaired piece is unique, because of the randomness with which ceramic shatters, and the irregular patterns formed that are enhanced with the use of metals. With this technique it's possible to create true and always differ-

ent works of art, each with its own story
and beauty, thanks to the unique cracks
formed when the object breaks, as if they
were wounds that leave different marks
on each of us.

Each one of us has brokenness that is unique to us and God sees it and knows exactly what He is going to make of it. Your brokenness will be something God will use, if you will let Him. Your redemptive story will be like a beautiful piece of kintsugi art that tells a story that no one else can tell, all for His glory. So start pouring out of expectation and keep pouring. He is creating something priceless. You are a stunning ezer warrior, scars and all.

Questions for Thought

1. Do you have circumstances that seem broken into a thousand pieces?
2. Has God made some kintsugi art out of shattered circumstances in your life?
3. Does it seem impossible for you to pour out from your brokenness?

Call to Action

This chapter may evoke emotions that you weren't prepared to face. Maybe the Lord is asking you to pour out forgiveness or kindness or respect when you really don't want to. Talk to Him about this. This may be hard, but ezers can do hard things. Trust that when you obey, God will start the miraculous on your behalf.

Chapter 10

Shadookie Happens, Keep Plowing

So Elijah went from there and found Elisha son of
Shaphat. He was plowing with twelve yoke of oxen,
and he himself was driving the twelfth pair. Elijah
went up to him and threw his cloak around him.

—1 Kings 19:19

Up to this point, we've had real talks, we've had deep exegesis talks, and we've had hard talks. Now it's time to talk
shadookie, because we all know shadookie happens. Let me
explain it with this verse from 1 Kings 19:19.

The prophet Elisha, the same prophet from our last
chapter, is the main character for this isolated verse. Typically,
I do not like to isolate a Bible verse because it is so easy to
take things out of context when a verse is isolated; however,
in this case, I feel it is perfectly in context for our purposes
here. You see, Elisha was minding his own business doing
what he always did: plow.

He was doing life. He was just plowing. The verse is
rather specific in telling us he was plowing with twelve yoke
of oxen. Don't mindlessly read the scripture. Everything is

there for a reason. When oxen are yoked together, there are two side by side in a yoke that is around both of their necks. If there were twelve yoke of oxen, that means there were twenty-four oxen. That's a lot of oxen.

Oxen are big animals, and big animals create big shadookie, and there's a lot of it. While you're giggling, stay with me. The last part of the verse says that Elisha himself was driving the twelfth pair, which means he was at the very back of twenty-four oxen. Every step he took was in shadookie. Some of my seasoned farming friends and family tell me that walking behind beasts like that and plowing a field causes the shadookie to sling up in all directions. Elisha would have been covered in it.

What's my point? Go back and look at the very first name mentioned in the verse—Elijah. The verse tells us that Elijah found Elisha right in the middle of his shadookie and went up to him and threw his cloak around him. This gesture was a symbol of Elijah passing his mantle or his anointing to Elisha. Elijah was saying by this gesture that Elisha was now his student and Elijah would be his mentor until the time the Lord took Elijah to glory. The cloak was most likely a wide fur wrap. It is also described in 2 Kings 1:8 as a garment of hair that was distinctive enough that King Ahab recognizes Elijah from its description alone. The passing of this hairy cloak was no small thing. Elisha's destiny, his purpose, his glory, was waiting for him on the other side of all that shadookie.

How does this apply to us as ezers? Oh, honey, if you haven't already seen yourself in this story, let me paint a picture for you. That's you and me walking behind the beasts of circumstances in our lives with shadookie being slung in our faces from all directions. The beasts can be bad decisions we made, decisions others made that affected us, a dying marriage, wayward children, insurmountable debt, pornography, betrayal, divorce, recent loss, sickness, past or present abuse, or the schemes of the enemy. The list could keep going. All of them are slinging shadookie at us, and we are just plowing through it not seeing a way out. We are just doing this life day in and day out, forgetting that we are mighty ezer warriors. Then the Almighty comes along on the other side of our shadookie. He comes to us and puts His cloak of righteousness on us and calls us out of the shadookie. This cloak of righteousness is so distinctive that our enemy recognizes it. When he sees us, he says, "She's an ezer with the DNA of the Holy One. She's wrapped in His righteousness. She belongs to the King."

Girls, if y'all were in this room with me right now, you would hear me shouting, "GLORY."

There's one last verse I want to look at. In 1 Kings 19:21, it says that Elisha left Elijah and took his twenty-four oxen and slaughtered all of them. He even burned the plowing equipment. Ezers, we have to take all the beasts that have been slinging shadookie at us, and we have to spiritually slaughter them and burn every last thing that reminds us of them and move forward into the purpose God has for us. God has made each one of us in His image, bearing His spiritual DNA, and He made us to have a unique glory. This glory is recognizable to the enemy and to others around us.

Sure, shadookie happens, but our glory and our divine purpose is just on the other side.

Questions for Thought

1. Do you have some shadookie that you're plowing through?
2. Do you believe that your glory and your purpose could be just on the other side of the shadookie that you're in?

Call to Action

Ask God to help you see Him in spite of the shadookie that you're plowing through. Recognize and know that He comes to you. He places His cloak of righteousness on you, and the enemy recognizes that cloak. Do not forget that.

Chapter 11

A Vast Army

As we bring this book to a close, let's do a little review. We have learned that our enemy is a big, fat liar and that he really hates us. We learned he wants to keep us bound in chains of bondage so that we can't do what an ezer was created to do, which is to be a strong, surrounding protection to our men and to those in our influence. We learned that our husbands and those around us are not our enemy. We learned that we are giant slayers marked with the initial of the Almighty Himself. We learned that there is beauty in our brokenness. We learned that shadookie happens and that we are an army of one. Wow! We've learned a lot.

Grab your Bible for one last Bible application. Go to Ezekiel 37:1–10. Oh, how I wish I could read this to you in person, but, alas, we must use our creative minds to insert ourselves into this moment by reading. Let's do this!

Ezekiel is being shown a vision by the Spirit of the Lord, which by the way, is the same Spirit that raised Christ from the dead and lives right now in those of us who trust in Jesus as our Savior. *Wow*, isn't that mind blowing!

The Spirit showed Ezekiel a valley with many dry bones on its floor. He asked Ezekiel, "Son of man, can these bones live?"

Ezekiel responded the way I think we all would have, "O Sovereign Lord, you alone know."

Then the Spirit told Ezekiel to prophesy to the dry bones and tell them, "Dry bones, hear the word of the Lord! I will make breath enter you, and you will come to life. I will attach tendons to you and make flesh come upon you and cover you with skin; I will put breath in you, and you will come to life. Then you will know that I am the Lord."

Let me pause here and say that I realize that the Spirit was speaking to Ezekiel about Israel, but I believe we are not taking too many liberties here to apply it to the valley of dead and dry-boned ezers! God's daughters have been lied to and trampled on to the extent that we have died to the knowledge of our true purpose and are lying dry on a valley floor. This is so exciting. Let's keep going.

In verse 7, Ezekiel prophesies as he was commanded, and as he was prophesying, there was a noise, a rattling sound, and the bones came together, bone to bone. Tendons and flesh appeared on them, and skin covered them, but there was no breath in them. Then the Spirit said to Ezekiel, "Prophesy to the breath; prophesy, son of man, and say to it, 'This is what the Sovereign Lord says: Come from the four winds, O breath, and breathe into these slain, *that they may live'*" (emphasis mine). So Ezekiel prophesied as he was commanded and breath entered them; they came to life and stood on their feet—a vast army!

Hear me, ezers! Hear me as if we are all together in one place standing to our feet. There is a noise in the spiritual atmosphere. A rattling sound of God's ezers coming to life. Our God is prophesying His breath into us. All the armies of one are now coming together to make a vast army of ezers that can change this world. It starts right there in your home. Stand your ground and surround and protect your people. Work together with your husband and your family like a well-oiled, Spirit-filled machine. Let's unite together and tell the enemy we will not take any more. There's a vast army on the move.

We are ezer, and we are glorious!

Final Questions for Thought

1.   Can you grasp that the same Spirit that spoke to Ezekiel and who raised Jesus from the dead is the same Spirit that lives in you?
2.   After reading this book, do you have a better understanding of your spiritual DNA?
3.   Do you feel new life coming into you now that you know you have been created to be an ezer?

Call to Action

If you have made it to the end of this book, whether alone or in a group, come before the Lord and pour out your heart to Him. Ask Him to drive the truth of His Word deep into your spirit and to help you to live this out. Girls, we cannot do this alone, but He has promised that He will empower us and equip us. He will never leave us nor forsake us. Run to Him, my sweet sister ezer. He is your everything; He is your King.

About the Author

Michelle Harrell is the founder of Glorious Marriage Revolution, a ministry that teaches women of all ages and seasons of life to know and confidently walk in the fierce beauty God has uniquely placed within them. Michelle is a lively and animated Bible teacher and speaker whose spiritual cup is filled when she sees people light up with an understanding of the Word as she teaches.

Michelle's glorious marriage began thirty-one years ago when she said "I do" to Brian, or as she likes to call him "her beautiful bald-headed man." They have two grown sons, Mack and Charlie, and a sweet puppy appropriately named Ezer. They currently live in Acworth, Georgia.